PET CARE FOR KIDS

HERMIT CRABS

BY KATHRYN STEVENS

The Child's World®

Published by The Child's World®
1980 Lookout Drive • Mankato, MN 56003-1705
800-599-READ • www.childsworld.com

Acknowledgments
The Child's World®: Mary Berendes, Publishing Director
The Design Lab: Kathleen Petelinsek, Design and Page Production

Photo Credits: Dwight Kuhn: 6, 7, 9, 11, 13, 15; Gator/Dreamstime.
com: front cover, 3, 24 (on sand); Juriah Mosin/Dreamstime.
com: 19; Kathleen Petelinsek: front cover, 1, 2, 12, 20 (food), 14;
iStockphoto.com/choicegraphx: back cover (brown); iStockphoto.
com/Kais Tolmats: front cover, back cover, 1, 3, 20, 22 (shells);
iStockphoto.com/Ross Elmi: 10; iStockphoto.com/Steve Goodwin:
front cover, 21 (in shell), back cover, 4, 18 (crawling); Lienkie/
Dreamstime.com: 5; Podius/Dreamstime.com: front cover, 20
(tank); Redmond Durrell/Alamy: 16; Richard Decker/Dreamstime.
com: front cover, 1, 22 (speckled); Steve Taylor/Alamy: 17; Ziablik/
Dreamstime.com: back cover (peeking)

Library of Congress Cataloging-in-Publication Data
Stevens, Kathryn, 1954–
    Hermit crabs / by Kathryn Stevens.
        p. cm. — (Pet care for kids)
    Includes index.
    ISBN 978-1-60253-184-0 (library bound : alk. paper)
    1. Hermit crabs as pets—Juvenile literature. I. Title. II. Series.
    SF459.H47S84 2009
    639'.67—dc22   2008040006

Printed in the United States of America
Mankato, Minnesota
December, 2009
PA02038

NOTE TO PARENTS AND EDUCATORS

The Pet Care for Kids series is written for children who want to be part of the pet experience but are too young to be in charge of pets themselves. These books are intended to provide a kid-friendly supplement to more detailed information adults need to know about choosing and caring for different types of pets. They can help youngsters learn how to live happily with the animals in their lives, and, with adults' help and supervision, grow into responsible animal caretakers later on.

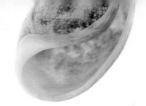

CONTENTS

HERMIT CRABS AS PETS

Hermit crabs are not cuddly. But they are interesting and fun to watch. They can make great pets. They take some special care. But they can live for a long time. Some live for 15 years—or even longer!

▸ Hermit crabs are strange-looking animals!

◂ This hermit crab is walking alone. But hermit crabs really like to live in groups.

BORROWED SHELLS

Most crabs have hard shells over their bodies. The shells help them stay safe. A hermit crab has a hard shell on its front half. Its back body parts are softer. The crab needs to keep the soft parts safe. So it uses old shells from other animals.

▶ This hermit crab is moving into a new shell. He looks different without one!

◀ This hermit crab has found another shell to move into.

A NICE HOME

Pet hermit crabs live in clear tanks called **aquariums**. A cover keeps the aquarium from drying out. The aquarium needs clean water and food dishes. It also needs extra shells for the crabs to wear. Some aquariums in cool places need heating pads.

▶ A cover keeps germs and other pets out of this aquarium. And it keeps the hermit crabs in!

Hermit crabs like to burrow and hide. The aquarium should have **moist** sand on the bottom. The crabs can dig and hide in it. Sometimes hermit crabs shed their old skins, or **molt**. They hide while they are doing this. Molting takes about a month.

▶ This hermit crab has a nice home. You can see a water dish, a food dish, and an empty shell. The white pill contains calcium (KAL-see-um).

◀ Hermit crabs need calcium to stay healthy. Eating bits of eggshell is one way for them to get calcium.

GOOD FOOD

Pet stores sell special foods for hermit crabs. Hermit crabs like healthy treats, too. Fruits and vegetables make good treats. Hermit crabs rest during the day. They are active at night. So evening is a good time to feed them.

▶ This hermit crab has come out to feed. Her owner has set out vegetables and other things to choose from.

◀ This flaky food is made just for hermit crabs.

GOOD HEALTH

Eating the right foods helps hermit crabs stay healthy. A clean aquarium also helps. Food and water dishes should be cleaned every day. Getting rid of old food is important. Sometimes the whole aquarium needs cleaning. It needs new sand, too.

▶ This hermit crab is taking a dip in his water dish. Some hermit crabs need to drink saltwater. It is salty like the sea. Others like saltwater for baths.

◀ Tap water can make hermit crabs ill. Special drops make the water safe.

SAFETY

Hermit crabs like to crawl around. It is fun to take them out of their aquarium. You can pick them up gently from the top. They can sit safely on your hand. They like to crawl around on smooth floors. They can get stuck in carpets.

▶ Careful handling keeps hermit crabs from getting hurt. And it keeps people from getting pinched!

◀ A hermit crab has ten legs. The back four hold onto the shell. The middle four walk. The front two have claws that pinch.

LOVING CARE

Hermit crabs are not warm and friendly like cats or dogs. But they still make good pets. And they still need good care. Hermit crabs' owners enjoy having them. They like seeing what the crabs do. Each hermit crab is different!

▶ This girl is gently picking up her hermit crab.

◀ Some stores sell painted shells for hermit crabs. But sometimes painted shells can be harmful. Many people think unpainted shells like this one are best.

NEEDS:

* a clean aquarium

* clean water

* moist sand

* places to hide

* good food

* extra shells

* safe things to climb on

DANGERS:

* getting hot, cold, or dry

* getting dropped

* soap or household cleaners

* bright sunlight

* pine or cedar wood

* deep water

* tap water

* saltwater made with table salt

BODIES:
Hermit crabs need to keep their bodies wet.

EYES:
Hermit crabs see very well. Their eyes are on long stalks.

FEELERS:
Hermit crabs have four feelers. They use them for smelling, feeling, and tasting.

CLAWS:
Hermit crabs have strong claws on their front legs.

SHELLS:
Hermit crabs need bigger shells as they grow.

GLOSSARY

aquariums (*uh-KWAYR-ee-ums*) Aquariums are clear tanks where animals can live.

moist (*MOYST*) Something that is moist has just a little water in it.

molt (*MOLT*) To molt is to lose old skin, fur, or feathers.

TO FIND OUT MORE

Books:

Binns, Tristan Boyer. *Hermit Crabs*. Keeping Unusual Pets series. Chicago, IL: Heinemann Library, 2004.

Nelson, Robin. *Pet Hermit Crab*. Classroom Pets series. Minneapolis, MN: Lerner Publications, 2003.

Video/DVD:

Paws, Claws, Feathers & Fins: A Kid's Guide to Happy, Healthy Pets. Goldhil Learning Series (Video 1993, DVD 2005).

Web Sites:

Visit our Web page for lots of links about pet care:
http://www.childsworld.com/links

Note to parents, teachers, and librarians: We routinely verify our Web links to make sure they are safe, active sites—so encourage your readers to check them out!

INDEX

ABOUT THE AUTHOR

Kathryn Stevens has authored and edited many books for young readers, including books on animals ranging from grizzly bears to fleas. She's a lifelong pet-lover and currently cares for a big, huggable pet-therapy dog named Fudge.